THE 2000 ELECTION

THE 2000 ELECTION

Ted Gottfried

The Millbrook Press
Brookfield, Connecticut

Published by The Millbrook Press, Inc.
2 Old New Milford Road
Brookfield, Connecticut 06804
www.millbrookpress.com

Library of Congress Cataloging-in-Publication Data
Gottfried, Ted.
The 2000 Election : thirty-six days of discord and doubt / Ted
Gottfried.
p. cm. (Headliners)
Includes bibliographical references and index.
ISBN 0-7613-2406-2 (lib. bdg.)
1. Presidents—United States—Election-2000—Juvenile
literature. 2. Electoral college—United States—Juvenile literature.
3. Elections—United States—Juvenile literature. [1. Presidents—
Election—2000. 2. Electoral college. 3. Elections.]
I. Title. II. Series.
JK526 2000I 324.973'0929—dc21 2001030971

Cover photographs courtesy of AP/Wide World Photos and
Reuters/Marc Serota/Archive Photos

Photographs courtesy of The Image Works: p. 6 (© David
Jennings); © AFP/Corbis: pp. 9, 11, 12, 50; Archive Photos:
pp. 13 (© Reuters/Mike Segar), 30 (© Reuters/Tami L. Chappell),
35 (© Reuters/Colin Braley); AP/Wide World Photos: pp. 16, 40,
42, 45, 49, 54; © Bettmann/Corbis: pp. 18, 22; Library of
Congress: pp. 24 (USZ62-7574), 28 (USZC4-3637); © Liaison/
Newsmakers/OnlineUSA: p. 32; © Reuters NewMedia Inc./
Corbis: pp. 36, 38

Contents

PRESIDENTIAL ELECTORS
FOR PRESIDENT
AND VICE PRESIDENT
(Vote ONCE)

1A
Republican
ELECTORS FOR
George W. Bush
FOR PRESIDENT
Dick Cheney
FOR VICE PRESIDENT

1B
Democratic
ELECTORS FOR
Al Gore
FOR PRESIDENT
Joe Lieber
FOR VICE PRES

Chapter 1

And the Winner Is . . . ?

For thirty-six days in November and December 2000, the presidential election seemed like a Hollywood suspense movie—lots of action, thrilling plot twists, colorful characters—but with the last reel misplaced, and no ending in sight. It was a cliffhanger, with the country hanging by its fingertips while the news media hyped up the drama. The audience—the American people—could do little but sit and wait, watch, and wonder.

Election Day, November 7, was supposed to be the climax of a hard-fought battle for the highest office in the land. The battle had begun with Governor George W. Bush of Texas and Vice President Albert Gore Jr. squaring off against determined opponents in the contest for the presidential nominations of their respective parties. In the Democratic race, Gore faced former Senator Bill Bradley of New Jersey, whose popularity as a star basketball player for the New York Knicks had propelled him into politics in 1978. The main issue between them was

Opposite:
When citizens cast their votes for president on November 7, 2000, they didn't know they were participating in what would become one of the most controversial elections in history. This voter in New York State selected Al Gore.

health care, with Bradley calling for massive reforms and Gore advocating a more gradual approach. While Bradley showed mounting support at first, it faded later and in the end he lost every state primary. Bradley's debates with the Vice President, however, revealed an image problem for Gore—he seemed to have a robot-like posture and a know-it-all manner. This would plague him when he faced Bush in their televised debates.

In the Republican race, Bush had a tougher primary battle against Senator John McCain of Arizona, a war hero who had been a prisoner of war in Vietnam. McCain's calls for campaign finance reform gained him wide support among Democrats as well as Republicans, leading him to claim that even if Bush won the nomination, he could not win the election. When McCain won the New Hampshire and Michigan primaries, Bush was in trouble. However, on March 7, Bush won seven of the eleven states in the Super Tuesday primaries, including the all-important high-delegate states of California and New York, and McCain dropped out of the race. Gore immediately made a pitch for reform-minded McCain Republicans to switch allegiance to the Democratic party.

Character and Personality

In August, the Republican and Democratic conventions officially nominated Bush and Gore as their presidential candidates. The main issue between them concerned the large surplus in the federal budget. Bush wanted to use it for a $1.3 trillion tax cut benefiting the rich as well as the poor. Gore favored only $500 billion in tax cuts, using much of the balance to improve education, beef up the military, and strengthen a variety of social programs. Other major differences between the two candidates concerned education, gun control, and abortion rights.

Before long, however, the media focused the public's attention on issues of character and personality. Gore was

Senator Joseph Lieberman of Connecticut was chosen as Al Gore's vice presidential running mate.

charged with having misused his position as Vice President to raise funds for the 1996 presidential campaign. Inevitably, some of the mud from the sex scandals that President Bill Clinton had been involved in had rubbed off on him. He was perceived as stiff, arrogant, and too smart for his own good. His early lead in the polls was soon eroded.

Bush profited from an easy going and friendly manner, but doubts were raised about his qualifications. In contrast to Gore, he had no experience in foreign policy. He fumbled questions from reporters and sometimes misstated facts. His hard-drinking youth came back to haunt him, costing him votes in the closing days of the campaign when it was reported that he had concealed a 1976 conviction for drunk driving.

Both Gore and Bush selected vice presidential candidates who would shore up their weaknesses. Gore chose Senator Joseph Lieberman of Connecticut, an Orthodox Jew and the first member of that religion ever to run for such high office. Deeply religious, Lieberman was able to reach out to fundamentalist Christians who were traditionally Republican. He had been the first prominent Democrat to condemn President Clinton's behavior as "immoral" during the Monica Lewinsky sex scandal, which led to Clinton's impeachment. Lieberman's integrity was unquestioned, and his warm personality compensated for Gore's relative stiffness.

Richard B. Cheney, chosen by Governor Bush as his running mate, had served under four Republican presidents. He had been a five-term congressman from Wyoming with a record of involvement in foreign policy. Cheney was Secretary of Defense under President George Bush, the governor's father, and had played an active role in the 1989 invasion of Panama and the Gulf War. He had also taken part in negotiating treaties and international agreements. Governor Bush would consult with Cheney and rely on his expertise.

Richard "Dick" Cheney's experience in foreign affairs was one reason
he was chosen as George W. Bush's vice presidential running mate.

The Candidates

ALBERT GORE JR.

The Democratic presidential candidate was born in 1948 in Carthage, Tennessee. His father, Albert Gore Sr., served three terms as U.S. senator from Tennessee. Pauline Gore, his mother, was a politically active lawyer.

Growing up, young Al lived half the time in a Washington, D.C., luxury hotel and half with tenant farmers in Tennessee on a Gore family farm with no indoor plumbing. He went on to Harvard University, graduating in 1969. A year later his father's outspoken opposition to the Vietnam War caused Gore Sr. to lose his bid for reelection to the Senate.

Although Gore Jr. also opposed the war, he enlisted in the army—either out of a sense of patriotic duty or because he hoped it would help revive his father's political career. That same year, 1970, he married his long-time sweetheart, Mary Elizabeth "Tipper" Aitcheson. They would have four children.

After Gore's discharge from the army, he worked on a Nashville newspaper while attending law school. Covering local government as a reporter stirred his interest in politics. In 1976 he ran for Congress and won. He served four terms as congressman and two terms as senator from Tennessee. In 1988, Gore ran for president, but lost the nomination to Governor Michael Dukakis of Massachusetts.

In 1989, Gore's six-year-old son, Albert III, was struck by a car and dragged fifty feet.

Al Gore

Gore was sure the boy was dead. However, he was revived, and after surgery and months of rehabilitation, he recovered. Gore has said the incident "completely changed my outlook on life."

In 1992, Bill Clinton chose Al Gore as his running mate. For the next eight years, Gore served as U.S. Vice President. On June 16, 1999, Albert Gore Jr. again announced his candidacy for the presidency of the United States.

GEORGE W. BUSH

Son of a president and grandson of a U.S. senator, George W. Bush is the oldest of five children. Born in New Haven, Connecticut, in 1946, George W., like his father, attended Phillips Academy in Massachusetts and Yale University. At Yale he was president of the Delta Kappa Epsilon fraternity.

After graduating from Yale, George W. served with the Texas Air National Guard, flying F-102s. Following his discharge, he worked with underprivileged children in Houston. Unfortunately, he also began drinking heavily. Bush himself says it was a time when he indulged in "irresponsible behavior."

His irresponsibility didn't last long, and Bush was soon at Harvard earning a degree in business administration. Soon after he returned to Texas in 1977, he married Laura Welch, a teacher and librarian. In 1978 he ran for Congress and lost by six votes. Over the next ten years he worked in the oil business and earned his first million dollars.

George W. helped manage his father's successful 1988 presidential campaign. When it was over, he returned to Texas, where he organized wealthy associates to bring baseball's Texas Rangers to Dallas. Bush effectively comanaged and promoted the team, boosting attendance.

In 1994, Bush ran for governor of Texas at the same time that his brother Jeb was

George W. Bush

running for governor of Florida. His opponent was the popular incumbent, Governor Ann Richards. When she called him "some jerk," he ignored the insult, focusing instead on such issues as welfare reform, education, and crime. He won with 53.5 percent of the vote and was re-elected in 1998.

In March 1999, George W. Bush announced that he was a candidate for president of the United States.

The Third-Party Threat

As Election Day approached, the polls had Bush and Gore running neck and neck. The media said the race was too close to call. Since citizens were voting for electors, rather than directly for president, there was concern that the 538 votes that make up the total of electors (the Electoral College; see next chapter) might split evenly, in which case it would be up to the House of Representatives to choose the next president. Adding to this concern, particularly for the Gore campaign, were those votes being drawn off by third-party candidates.

The threat to Gore came from Ralph Nader and his Green party. Nader had strong backing among conservationists in the Northwest and was gaining support from labor organizations. Pre-election polls showed Nader also building support among liberal Democrats. In particular the Democrats feared that he might draw enough votes away from Gore in Minnesota and Wisconsin to make Bush the winner in those states. During the last days of the campaign, this possibility pushed the Democrats into expending much time and money to appeal to Nader supporters to switch to Gore.

Bush faced a less serious threat posed by Pat Buchanan and the Reform party. The party had been formed by Ross Perot, who, in 1992, had received an impressive 19 percent of the national vote for president. However, Buchanan's negative remarks about Israel and the Holocaust made him unacceptable to many Reform party conservatives. There had been a power struggle inside the party, and Buchanan had nothing like the support Perot had enjoyed. The votes he might draw away from Bush among fundamentalist Christians were not considered enough to be significant. Buchanan, however, did have an unanticipated and unintended effect on the election in Florida.

A Night to Remember

At 7:47 P.M. Eastern Standard Time on Election Day, NBC, CBS, ABC, CNN, Fox, and the Associated Press declared Gore the winner in Florida. At that time Bush had 54 electoral votes to Gore's 28. Thirteen minutes later the polls closed in many Eastern states and the networks projected winners in twelve states, including the high-delegate states of Texas, Michigan, and Illinois. That made the count almost a tie, giving Bush 121 delegates and Gore 119. At 9:54 P.M., the networks announced that they had been mistaken: Gore had not won Florida; the count was now 185 for Bush, 167 for Gore, with 186 electoral votes not determined yet.

Over the next four hours, as those 186 votes were tallied, the race was close, with Gore picking up a slight, but significant lead. What followed was a comedy of errors. At 2:18 A.M., the media announced that Bush had won Florida's 25 electoral votes, giving him the 271 needed to capture the presidency. In Nashville, Vice President Gore called Governor Bush at the Governor's Mansion in Austin, Texas, and conceded the election. After congratulating Bush, he set out in his limousine to address a gathering of his rain-drenched supporters at the Nashville War Memorial Plaza. En route, Gore received an urgent message to call a campaign strategist in Florida.

The news was that Bush's 50,000-vote lead in Florida had shrunk to 6,000, with precincts favorable to Gore still not counted. When Gore's motorcade reached the plaza, he called Bush back. He told him that the race was now too close to call and that there would be an automatic recount, and so he had decided to wait it out.

"You mean to tell me, Mr. Vice President, you're retracting your concession?" Bush, who was preparing his victory speech, was incredulous.

"You don't have to be snippy about it," Gore replied.

The *Columbus* (Ohio) *Dispatch*, like other newspapers and media throughout the country, changed its headline as election results trickled in. The front page on the right shows an early edition of the November 8 paper, while the front page on the left shows a later edition of the same day's paper.

Bush then said that his brother Jeb, the governor of Florida, had just assured Bush that he had won Florida.

"Let me explain something," Gore replied. "Your younger brother is not the ultimate authority on this."

Shortly after 4 A.M., the networks announced that the outcome of the vote in Florida was undecided. It was their third call regarding Florida. The media had embarrassed itself. Now the count was 246 for Bush, 249 for Gore. Florida's 25 electoral votes would decide the election.

Howard Chandler Christy

Chapter 2

The Electoral College

Before the 2000 election, many citizens assumed that the United States was a nation governed by majority rule. It is not, and it never has been. Our country is governed by proportional representation, a system requiring that federal government offices be distributed among competing parties, or candidates, in a manner proportionate to the votes of the people. This was decided by the Constitutional Convention of 1787–1788.

Proposals and Compromises

At that time, the United States was a new nation made up of thirteen large and small states protective of their own rights and powers, and suspicious of a central national government. The nation's four million people were spread out over a large area. Transportation was by horse-and-buggy, and there was no telephone or tele-

Opposite:
How to elect the new nation's president was one of the issues debated by the attendees of the Constitutional Convention in 1787. The man who would become the first president, George Washington, stands on the platform.

graph for spreading information. National political campaigns were impractical.

The Constitutional Convention considered various methods of electing the president. It rejected a proposal by founding father Alexander Hamilton that the president and senators serve life terms. Delegates also dismissed the idea of electing a president by majority vote because most citizens would not have sufficient knowledge of candidates outside their own state to choose wisely. They would vote for a "favorite son," and no candidate would emerge with a majority. The small states feared that they would always be outvoted by the large states. A suggestion that members of the state legislatures select the president was dismissed because of fear that this would give the state legislators too much direct influence over the president and undermine the power of the new-born federal government.

Finally, a so-called Committee of Eleven in the Convention proposed an indirect election of the president through a College of Electors. It was based on procedures followed by the Roman Republic in earlier times. When this proposal was adopted as Article II, Section I of the United States Constitution, a key provision was that individual state legislatures should decide how the Electors should be chosen.

At that time, these state legislators were themselves chosen by some form of popular vote decided upon by the legislature itself. The legislature also set the qualifications for voting. In all states the qualifications excluded Native Americans, slaves, free African-Americans, and women. In nearly all states, men without property had no right to vote. All of those involved in the appointment of Electors to vote for a president and vice president were well-off white males. For many years after the adoption of the Constitution, most state legislatures appointed the Electors directly. Citizens did not vote for the Electors who would choose the president.

Electors were required to meet in their individual states, rather than coming together in the nation's capital. Each Elector was required to cast two votes for president. One of the two had to be for someone outside the Elector's home state. The votes would then be sent to the Senate to be counted. The candidate with the majority was to become president, and the candidate with the next highest number of Electoral votes would become vice president. If there was a tie, the House of Representatives would choose the president. The delegation from each state in the House would have one vote. The vice presidency would go to the candidate who had gotten the second highest number of Electoral votes. If that, too, was a tie, the Senate would decide between those two candidates.

The Twelfth Amendment

In 1800, the design of the Electoral College was severely tested. In that election, the Democratic-Republican party defeated the Federalists. The Democratic-Republican candidates for president and vice president were Thomas Jefferson and Aaron Burr. The Electors, however, had not indicated which of the two should be president and which vice president. When the Electors gave each an equal number of Electoral votes, the matter was referred to the House of Representatives to decide the tie. The debate in the House generated a great deal of ill feeling and was settled only after some very unethical political deals had been made. The disgust it provoked led to the hasty adoption of the Twelfth Amendment to the Constitution.

The Twelfth Amendment said that the Electors had to cast one vote for president and a separate vote for vice president, rather than casting two votes for president with the runner-up automatically selected as vice president.

Ballots and Bullets

Aaron Burr was credited with the overwhelming victory in New York State that carried the presidential election of 1800 for the Democrat-Republican party. When he and Thomas Jefferson tied in the Electoral vote for president and the decision was thrown into the House of Representatives, the standoff lasted through thirty-six bitter votes. Federalist Alexander Hamilton led the fight against Burr and finally succeeded in securing the presidency for Jefferson.

Hamilton's opposition to Burr stemmed from a grudge that had begun nine years earlier when Burr had defeated Hamilton's father-in-law in a senatorial election. Now, with Burr serving as Jefferson's vice president, the grudge festered. It came to a head in 1804 when Burr ran for governor of New York State and lost. He was also blocked from running for a second term as vice president with Jefferson. When he learned that Hamilton had circulated charges against him that insulted his character and honor, Burr demanded an explanation. When Hamilton refused to give him one, Burr challenged him to a duel.

Dueling was illegal in New York State, so the two fought in Weehawken, New Jersey. Burr's bullet killed Hamilton. Warrants were issued for Burr's arrest in two states. He fled to Philadelphia and then further south, where Hamilton was hated because of his politics and Burr was cheered and toasted for bringing about his death.

Not long after the duel, a federal judge faced impeachment charges. His trial was held in the United States Senate. It was presided over by Vice President Aaron Burr.

Aaron Burr

With a two-party system not yet established, there might be three, four, or more candidates for the highest office. Therefore, when no candidate had a majority in the Electoral College, the Twelfth Amendment designated the House of Representatives to select the president from among the three highest vote-getters. As before, each state delegation in the House had one vote. When there was no majority for vice president, the Senate was to assign the office to one of the two highest vote-getters. All other features of the original Electoral College remained the same.

These reform measures favored the election of a president and vice president from the same party. The changes seemed slight, but they altered the Electoral College in one important way. They encouraged the growth of political parties and influenced them to seek power through campaigning for votes, as well as through their participation in government. The reforms forced the parties to formulate principles and programs, rather than relying on the personal popularity of their candidates.

Flaws and Controversies

In the election of 1824, the Twelfth Amendment was put to the test. There were four presidential candidates— Andrew Jackson, John Quincy Adams, William Crawford, and Henry Clay. Each represented a different faction within the Democratic-Republican party. None received a majority of votes in the Electoral College. Andrew Jackson, who received the greatest number of votes cast in the general election, also received the most votes in the Electoral College. Nevertheless, because he didn't have a majority, under the Twelfth Amendment the selection of the president was determined by the House of Representatives, which chose John Quincy Adams. It was the first time (but not the last) that a candidate with the

When John Quincy Adams beat Andrew Jackson to become president in 1824,
it was the first time that a candidate with the highest number of popular votes
failed to become president. Jackson went on to be elected president four years later.

highest popular vote failed to be elected president.

In 1836, the Whig party ran three different presidential candidates—William Henry Harrison, Daniel Webster, and Hugh White—in different parts of the country. Each was popular in his own region, and the idea was that this would result in a Whig majority in the Electoral College, which would then decide on one of the three for president. It didn't work. The rival Democratic-Republican candidate, Martin Van Buren, won a majority of Electors and became president. But that wasn't the end of it. In the Electoral College, Van Buren's vice presidential running mate, Richard Johnson, was blocked by the Whigs from obtaining enough votes to be elected vice president. In the end, the vice presidential choice was made by the Senate, and Johnson was finally confirmed.

Horace Greeley, the Democratic candidate in the 1872 election, died during the period between the popular vote and the casting of ballots by the Electoral College. Three of the Electors voted for him anyway. Other Democratic Electors split their votes among several other Democratic candidates. Republican Ulysses S. Grant, however, won a majority of Electors and became president.

In the period after the Civil War, Reconstruction resulted in two sets of electoral votes from South Carolina, Louisiana, and Florida in the election of 1876. The reborn Democratic party sent Electors to the Electoral College pledged to Samuel J. Tilden. Republicans, their numbers swelled by new African-American voters, sent Electors pledged to Rutherford B. Hayes. When the Electoral College couldn't decide between the slates, the debate shifted to Congress, where members of both parties threatened to seize the government by force. A pistol shot was fired at Tilden through the window of his home where he was seated at dinner with his family.

How the System Works Today

The Electoral College consists of Electors from each state equal in number to the number of the state's members in the House of Representatives plus two—one for each senator. Because of the redrawing of congressional districts due to population shifts, the number of each state's Electors may change from one election to the next. Political parties name slates of Electors pledged to their candidate. Citizens voting for a presidential candidate are actually voting for one of these slates.

A "winner-takes-all" system decrees that the candidate receiving the most votes in the state as a whole receives *all* of that state's electoral votes. The legislature validates the winning slate as the state's Electors. Acting collectively, Electors from each state select the president and vice president.

If there is a tie vote in the Electoral College, the House of Representatives selects the president. The representatives from each state vote collectively, casting only one vote for that state. They may determine that a candidate who tied for the electoral vote, but lost by a sizable margin in the popular vote, will be president. Meanwhile, the Senate chooses the vice president. The hundred senators are presided over by the present vice president. In case of a tie, his vote will decide his successor.

In the House, however, a 25–25 tie is possible. In that case, the vice president chosen by the Senate becomes acting president. However, if the balance of power in the House of Representatives is changed after two years by the midterm election, the House might then name a president from either party. The acting president would then revert back to his role as vice president. This is an unlikely sequence of events. However, if Election 2000 has taught us anything, it is that in politics, if something can happen, sooner or later it will happen.

WA
11

MT
3

ND
3

MN
10

MI

NH
4

VT
3

ME
4

OR
7

ID
4

SD
3

WI
11

MI
18

NY
33

MA
12

WY
3

IA
7

RI
4

NV
4

NE
5

IL
22

IN
12

OH
21

PA
23

CT
8

NJ
15

CA
54

UT
5

CO
8

KS
6

MO
11

KY
8

WV
5

VA
13

DE
3

MD
10

DC
2

AZ
8

NM
5

OK
8

AR
6

TN
11

NC
14

HI
4

AK
3

MS
7

AL
9

GA
13

SC
8

LA
9

TX
32

FL
25

THE 2000 ELECTION

States and number of electoral
votes won by George W. Bush

States and number of electoral
votes won by Al Gore

Samuel J. Tilden (left) ran a successful campaign,
but he lost the presidency with Congress's decision to accept
the electors of his opponent, Rutherford B. Hayes.

Congress finally appointed a fifteen-member commission to resolve which set of Electors was legitimate. The commission decided by one vote to accept Hayes's Electors. Tilden had a majority of popular votes, but Hayes was officially designated president on March 2, 1877—almost four months after the votes were cast. Two days later he was sworn in.

Eleven years later, in 1888, Benjamin Harrison carried the Electoral College and became president although Grover Cleveland won the popular vote. That conflict was resolved more smoothly because the year before, 1887, Congress had enacted legislation that delegated to each state the final authority to decide between competing slates of Electors. Only the designated officer in each state could validate its choice of Electors. That legislation was still in effect in November 2000. At that time, the person designated to grant such validation in Florida was Secretary of State Katherine Harris.

Chapter 3

The Standoff

In the days following November 7, 2000, more and more journalists, lawyers, politicians, and constitutional experts were propelled into the spotlight of Election 2000. There was a frantic attempt to make sense of the intricacies of the Electoral College, the fine points of Florida election law, the designs of ballots and voting machines, and the roles of election officials, canvassing commissioners, manual vote counters, the legislature, the courts, and Florida Secretary of State Katherine Harris. The first hurdle was the butterfly ballot.

The Palm Beach Story

The punch-hole butterfly ballot had been designed by Palm Beach election supervisor Theresa LePore, a Democrat, to make it easier for elderly citizens with vision problems to vote. The design, however, had defeated the intention.

Opposite:
Reverend Jesse Jackson (right) leads a demonstration in Tallahassee, Florida, on December 13 to protest the U.S. Supreme Court decision not to allow a recount of controversial ballots.

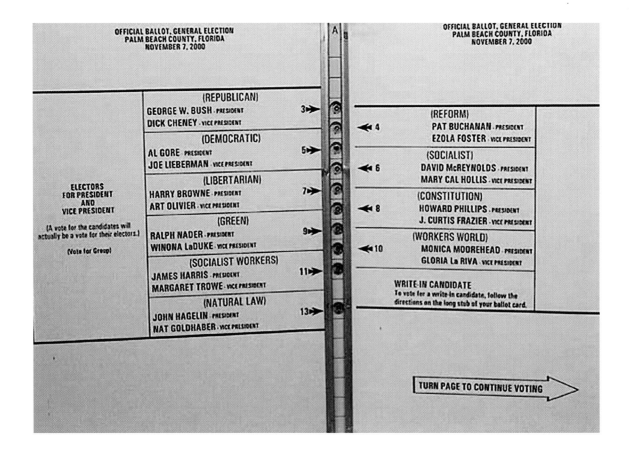

OFFICIAL BALLOT, GENERAL ELECTION
PALM BEACH COUNTY, FLORIDA
NOVEMBER 7, 2000

(REPUBLICAN)
GEORGE W. BUSH - PRESIDENT   3►
DICK CHENEY - VICE PRESIDENT

(DEMOCRATIC)
AL GORE - PRESIDENT   5►
JOE LIEBERMAN - VICE PRESIDENT

(LIBERTARIAN)
HARRY BROWNE - PRESIDENT   7►
ART OLIVIER - VICE PRESIDENT

(GREEN)
RALPH NADER - PRESIDENT   9►
WINONA LaDUKE - VICE PRESIDENT

(SOCIALIST WORKERS)
JAMES HARRIS - PRESIDENT   11►
MARGARET TROWE - VICE PRESIDENT

(NATURAL LAW)
JOHN HAGELIN - PRESIDENT   13►
NAT GOLDHABER - VICE PRESIDENT

ELECTORS
FOR PRESIDENT
AND
VICE PRESIDENT

(A vote for the candidates will
actually be a vote for their electors.)

(Vote for Group)

OFFICIAL BALLOT, GENERAL ELECTION
PALM BEACH COUNTY, FLORIDA
NOVEMBER 7, 2000

(REFORM)
◄ 4   PAT BUCHANAN - PRESIDENT
EZOLA FOSTER - VICE PRESIDENT

(SOCIALIST)
◄ 6   DAVID McREYNOLDS - PRESIDENT
MARY CAL HOLLIS - VICE PRESIDENT

(CONSTITUTION)
◄ 8   HOWARD PHILLIPS - PRESIDENT
J. CURTIS FRAZIER - VICE PRESIDENT

(WORKERS WORLD)
◄ 10   MONICA MOOREHEAD - PRESIDENT
GLORIA La RIVA - VICE PRESIDENT

WRITE-IN CANDIDATE
To vote for a write-in candidate, follow the
directions on the long stub of your ballot card.

TURN PAGE TO CONTINUE VOTING ►

The Butterfly ballot

There were two facing columns of candidates' names, with the right-hand column slightly staggered so that its top was about a half-inch below the top of the left-hand column. Although Florida law said that paper ballots "must have a space for the voters to mark their choice on the right," punch-hole ballots were only required to conform to that standard "as nearly as practicable." The punch-holes ran down the center of the butterfly ballot, with arrows to both the right and left of the spine. Bush and Cheney's names were at the top of the left-hand column with Gore and Lieberman's names directly below them. The names of Buchanan and his vice presidential running mate, Ezola Foster, were at the top of the right-hand column. The first punch-hole meant a vote for

Bush, the second for Buchanan, and the third for Gore. Since the Democratic slate was listed directly below the Republican slate, however, it was easy to assume that the second punch-hole down would be for Gore, when it was actually for Buchanan.

On November 8, the day after Election Day, three voters filed suit to throw out the Palm Beach results because the county's ballots were "deceptive, confusing and/or misleading." Reform party candidate Pat Buchanan had received more than 3,000 votes in Palm Beach, one-fifth of the total votes he got in all of Florida's sixty-seven counties. Palm Beach had a large majority of registered Democrats, some of whom claimed that they meant to vote for Gore, but voted for Buchanan by mistake. Buchanan himself said that he believed many of his Palm Beach votes had been intended for Gore. Soon, led by African-American poitical leader the Reverend Jesse Jackson, Democratic protesters rallied, chanting "RE-VOTE! RE-VOTE! RE-VOTE!" and waving signs with anti-Bush slurs.

Over 19,000 butterfly ballots were not counted because they had been punched twice, many by Gore voters who realized their mistake after punching the hole for Buchanan and then punched a second hole for Gore. Other ballots were disallowed because they had not been punched through cleanly so the scanners that counted the votes could not read them. On November 12, Palm Beach electoral officials agreed to a hand recount of all of the county's 462,657 ballots.

The Hand Count Controversy

Democratic party demands for hand recounts in four counties—Palm Beach, Miami-Dade, Broward, and Volusia—followed a machine recount of all of Florida's nearly six million votes. Florida law made the machine

Pregnant Dimples and Hanging Chads

The dispute over hand counts focused on chads. A chad is the tiny piece of paper forced out in punch-card balloting, the system used in fifteen Florida counties. Other counties used cards that voters marked with a pencil. Both types were read by machine scanners, which tallied each person's vote.

Machine scanners reject ballots that they cannot read. Florida punch-card scanners rejected 1.5 percent of the ballots run through them. Scanners for hand-checked ballots rejected only 0.3 percent. Florida punch-card scanners were over thirty years old. They were used mostly in Democratic counties.

Punch-card devices are used in 34 percent of elections in the United States—more than any other voting system. A voter receives a ballot when entering the voting booth. There are no names on it. The ballot is inserted in the punch-card voting device and locked into place by two pins. A list of candidates attached to the left side of the device is folded over the ballot. Next to each name there is a hole. Using a stylus, the voter punches through the hole next to the name of the preferred candidate.

The voting device is a box with a flat cover, or template. The template has holes lining up with the holes in the list of candidates folded over the ballot. The holes lead to rubber funnels, narrow at the top and wide at the bottom to allow the chads to fall cleanly into the box. Instructions tell the voter to "hold the punch straight up and push down through the card next to the preferred candidate's name."

After voting, the card is removed from the device, put into a locked ballot box, and later read by the punch-hole scanner. If a chad blocks a hole, the scanner will not count it.

It was claimed that Palm Beach machines had not been cleaned of old chads, leading to chad buildup in the funnels, which stopped subsequent chads from separating. After repeated use of the punch-hole device, the holes in the candidate list might not line up with the template holes, which would also prevent the chad from separating. Finally, older people in Palm Beach County could

A worker in Broward County applies the "sunshine test" to a butterfly ballot.

have difficulty pushing the chad out.

When the hand count of punch-card ballots began on November 11, election officials used the "sunshine" rule to determine the intent of voters: They held a ballot up to see if a sliver of light showed through. Ridicule from the media and Republican protests led to that standard being discarded. It was replaced by a 1990 Palm Beach County standard that said sunlight could be used as a guide, but votes would be counted only if a chad was hanging. By that time, the hand count had added 55 votes to the Gore total, reducing Bush's Florida lead to only 288 votes.

Now a so-called "pregnant chad," or dimpled chad, which had been pressured, but wasn't hanging, could not be counted as a vote. But what constituted a hanging chad? Only those dangling by one corner with three corners punched out could be counted, said the Republicans. Democrats insisted that swinging chads with two corners attached, and even tri-chads with three corners holding, should be counted.

It had become a legal question that was up to the courts to decide. But could they?

Workers in Palm Beach County examine and hand count controversial butterfly ballots.

recount automatic in close elections. On the morning after Election Day, Bush had led Gore by 1,784 votes. After the machine recount, his lead had shrunk to 327 votes. The Democrats claimed that only hand recounts of the votes that the scanning machines had been unable to read could provide an honest count. Theodore Olson, a Bush lawyer who opposed hand recounts, called them "selective, standardless, subjective, unreliable and inherently biased." Bruce Rogow, a Gore campaign lawyer, granted that manual recounts were "messy," but added, "That is democracy."

Meanwhile, Palm Beach County election supervisor Carol Roberts vowed to count every vote. In response to the suggestion that the vote counters wait for a ruling from Secretary of State Harris, she responded, "I'm not asking for an opinion. I'm asking for a vote." Shrugging off the legality of the hand count, Roberts added, "I'm ready to go to jail."

In Palm Beach County and Broward County, judges ruled that hand counts could go forward. On November 13, Harris ruled that all counting must stop by 5 P.M. the following day. The next day she certified the election results, minus the overseas absentee ballots (expected to be favorable to Bush), in effect sealing Bush's victory in Florida and in the national election.

However, confusion mounted. Florida's Democratic state attorney general, Bob Butterworth, advised that the hand counts were legal and could continue. A circuit court judge ruled that Harris's deadline was legal, but that she could not arbitrarily disregard hand count tallies that came in after the deadline. Harris then gave counties until 2 P.M. the following day, November 15, to submit reasons why the hand count should continue. Broward stopped its hand count, and Democrats sued the county. However, on November 15, Broward joined with Dade and Palm Beach counties in submitting reasons why the hand count should resume. Harris, rejecting their arguments, petitioned the Florida Supreme Court to suspend all hand counts. That same day, November 15, Broward County reversed itself and resumed its hand count. On November 16, the Florida Supreme Court denied Harris's petition and ruled that hand counts could proceed.

The Shifting Stands

Inconsistency and confusion created chaos. While Republicans challenged the accuracy of hand counts in Florida, in Texas they demanded a hand count in a con-

The Lady in the Lightning

In the raging storm following Election Day, Florida's secretary of state, Katherine Harris, faced the lightning flashes of camera bulbs and TV spots. She announced that the "counting and recounting of votes cast on Election Day must end by 5 P.M. November fourteen, which is tomorrow." In effect, she was giving Florida's electoral votes and the presidency to George W. Bush.

Six years before, Katherine Harris had been performing the chicken dance in a cabaret and coaxing the audience to participate. Prior to that she worked in real estate. Some accused her of being "a country-club lightweight" whose only experience making decisions was choosing between "pearls or diamonds."

Such choices came naturally to her. Harris inherited roughly $7 million from her cattle baron grandfather. However, she was not a lightweight. She held a master's degree in public administration from Harvard. Before being elected secretary of state, she spent four years in the state Senate, leading an economic development committee that attracted business to the state and developed jobs.

As Florida's secretary of state, Harris continued on that track but was controversial. She was criticized for spending $100,000 of the taxpayers' money on business trips to New York, Brazil, and Australia. The media attacked her for calling on the Florida Highway Patrol to provide a two-and-a-half-hour escort back to Tallahassee when fog grounded her state-owned plane. Because she was cochair of George W. Bush's Florida campaign, her halting of the vote count was called partisan.

A 1998 change in the Florida constitution eliminated Harris's job as secretary of state in 2002. Democrats predicted that she might be appointed an ambassador by President Bush. Others believed that she wanted to be secretary of agriculture.

Doubts about Harris's electoral decisions remain. Was she playing politics, or had she "no choice but to follow the law"? It's one more question left hanging by the election of 2000.

Florida's Secretary of State Katherine Harris

gressional race that the Democrats claimed to have won by 2,080 votes. The mandatory Texas hand count had been signed into law two years earlier by Governor George W. Bush. Meanwhile, in Seminole County, Florida, the very Democrats who had been insisting that "every vote must be counted" had filed a lawsuit to disallow 4,700 Bush votes on the grounds that Republicans had tampered with some voters' absentee ballot applications.

Another controversy erupted over Florida's 3,626 overseas ballots. Bush had gained 1,380 to Gore's 750 in the overseas vote. However, Democrats persuaded officials to bar 1,420 of the 3,626 ballots for technical reasons. Many of them did not have postmarks, which were required by Florida law. Most of the disputed ballots were from men and women in military service. Republicans accused Democrats of having the ballots thrown out because voters in the armed services favored Bush over Gore. Democrats said they simply wanted the votes accepted or rejected according to Florida law. Senator Bob Kerrey sarcastically asked, if Republicans wanted to count the votes of "people who were treated unfairly" because of Florida state regulations, "are they willing to do the same thing for an 85-year-old who simply did not have the strength to punch through a punch card?"

Ageism was not the only form of discrimination being charged. The National Association for the Advancement of Colored People (NAACP) held hearings regarding racial bias in the Florida elections. Black people claimed that they had been required to provide documents not asked of white voters. Latinos said they had not had access to legally required translators. The Justice Department investigated the claims after a suit was filed in federal court on behalf of a black Tampa resident who said he was turned away from the polls because he didn't have a driver's license.

The Nader Factor

Democratic fears that Ralph Nader's Green party would siphon off votes from the Gore ticket proved justified. What wasn't anticipated was that the Nader vote would cost Gore the state of Florida. On Election Day, the Green party racked up 2 percent of the ballots cast in Florida for a total of 96,837 votes. At the same time, Bush was leading Gore by 1,725 votes.

How many of Nader's votes would Gore have gotten if Nader had not run? Nationwide, exit polls showed that 47 percent of Nader voters would have voted for Gore in a two-man race. Had that been true of even a small percentage of Florida's Nader voters, Bush's lead would have been swept away.

Nader had needed 5 percent of the national vote to be eligible for federal matching funds in the 2004 election. He got 2.6 million votes, about 3 percent. To his followers, he had waged a heroic uphill battle. To loyal Democrats, he would always be the spoiler who cost them the election. To Republicans, he was a godsend.

Ralph Nader addresses a group of students at the University of Southern Maine during an election-day rally.

All of these controversies were moving through the lower state and federal courts. No matter who prevailed in any of them, they would be appealed to higher courts. This situation led both parties to interesting positions. Traditionally, in recent years, Republicans had been strong on states' rights, while Democrats believed that the federal government was the ultimate authority over the states. Now, however, as the Florida election moved into the courts, the Democrats would hold that decisions by the Florida Supreme Court were final and that there was no federal right to override them. Republicans, on the other hand, would insist that the United States Supreme Court must have the final word. The battle of the justices was about to begin.

Chapter 4

Decisions, Decisions, Decisions . . .

In the end, the election would be determined by the courts. Two judicial systems were involved. The Florida state system is made up of sixty-seven county courts whose decisions can be challenged in the twenty Florida circuit courts. Judgments in the circuit courts can be appealed to five Florida district courts. Appeals can go as high as the seven-member Florida Supreme Court, which is the state's highest legal authority.

The federal court system consists of ninety-four district courts nationwide, three of which are in Florida. District courts are where cases subject to federal jurisdiction are filed. Their decisions can be overturned by one of the thirteen U.S. courts of appeal. The court of appeals overseeing Florida is in Atlanta, Georgia. The final authority is the nine-member United States Supreme Court, which is also the only body that can nullify decisions by state supreme courts such as Florida's.

Opposite:
Boxes of ballots from Miami-Dade and Palm Beach counties arrive at the Florida Supreme Court to be used as evidence.

"Judge Not, Lest Ye Be Judged"

A Palm Beach County circuit court was thrust into the election controversy immediately after Election Day when the first of six suits contesting the butterfly ballot was brought. On November 13, the six were consolidated into one suit assigned to Judge Stephen A. Rapp. However, Judge Rapp had to remove himself from the case after it was revealed that he had told a lawyer that "anyone who mistakenly voted for the wrong candidate had no legal right to appeal." Circuit judge Jorge Labarga, who eventually heard the case, decided that it was "not legally possible to have a revote or a new election" no matter how misleading the butterfly ballots had been.

Meanwhile, on November 11, Bush's lawyers had filed suit in federal court in Miami to halt all hand counts because there was "no uniform standard" governing them. On November 13, U.S. district court judge Donald M. Middlebrooks, a Democratic appointee, rejected their argument on the grounds that election standards were a state, not a federal, issue. On November 14, it was revealed that Judge Middlebrook had donated over $19,000 to Democratic causes.

When the Florida Supreme Court backed up Judge Middlebrook, ruling that hand counts could proceed, the Bush forces appealed in the federal court of appeals in Atlanta. Gore's lawyers repeated the argument that federal courts had no jurisdiction. The court of appeals dismissed the Bush claim.

During the three preceding days, three other Republican suits had been dismissed by various courts. On November 14, an action filed by three Brevard County residents to have hand counts declared unconstitutional was dismissed by the U.S. district court in Orlando. That same day a federal circuit court judge refused to halt the Broward County hand count. A day

Heart to Heart

On November 22, Republican vice presidential candidate Dick Cheney was hospitalized with chest pains. Initially, George Washington University Hospital officials released "misinformation," according to *The New York Times* and other media sources, that led them to conclude that Cheney had not had a heart attack. Bush campaign officials repeated the hospital's assessment. Eventually, however, it was revealed that Cheney had indeed had a heart attack, his fourth. A previous one had required quadruple bypass surgery. This time a dangerously blocked artery had been opened and a device inserted to keep it open. Inevitably, questions were raised as to Cheney's ability to stand up to the stresses of the job he was seeking.

Before leaving George Washington University Hospital,
Dick Cheney assured the media that he is in fine health and
fit to do the job of vice president.

later, a Florida state circuit court also refused to stop the Broward hand count.

A suit by the Gore forces accused Secretary of State Harris of not using "appropriate discretion" before dismissing counties' requests to submit hand-counted ballots after the original deadline. On November 17, the state circuit court rejected the suit. Gore appealed to the Florida Supreme Court, which prohibited Harris from certifying election results until it decided the case. The good news for Gore was that Miami-Dade County decided to proceed with a full hand recount.

Twenty-Five Lawsuits, and Counting

The good news was short-lived. On November 22, the Florida Supreme Court extended the deadline for Secretary Harris to accept hand recount totals, but only up to the morning of November 27. That wasn't long enough for Miami-Dade, which once again stopped its recount. However, recounts went ahead in Palm Beach and Broward counties.

Republicans were enraged that the Florida Supreme Court had set no standards for counting chads. Republican senator Orrin Hatch of Utah charged that the court's Democratic majority had found a way "to give the election to Gore." However, after Gore's lawyers asked the state appeals court to order Miami-Dade to resume its hand count and the request was denied, the Florida Supreme Court also refused to compel Miami-Dade to count ballots.

Meanwhile, the question of the 1,420 overseas absentee ballots that had been set aside uncounted because they lacked a proper postmark had been decided. Although they were presumed to heavily favor Bush, Florida Democratic attorney general Bob Butterworth ordered all the state's counties to "count overseas ballots which are from qualified military electors, and which bear no postmark, if the ballot is signed and dated no later than the date of the election."

On November 26, Secretary of State Harris, adding in the overseas ballots, declared Bush the winner in Florida by 537 votes. Democrats challenged this result and vowed to fight it in the courts. By now there were twenty-five Florida lawsuits involving the election.

A Very Dramatic Moment

Media attention focused on two cases. The first was Bush's appeal to overturn the Florida Supreme Court decision to allow the hand counts to proceed while extending the deadline for including their results. On November 24, the U.S. Supreme Court agreed to hear this appeal, and on December 1 the nine justices heard arguments from both sides. Questions of jurisdiction and constitutionality were raised, but not settled. On December 4, the court unanimously "avoided a definitive ruling" by sending the case back to the Florida Supreme Court, asking it to clarify its decision.

The second case was brought by Gore's forces to challenge certification of Bush's victory in Florida. On December 2, the trial opened in Tallahassee, the state capital. A Republican appointee, Judge N. Sanders Sauls of Leon County Circuit Court, presided. Gore attorney David Boies argued that 14,000 disputed ballots from Miami-Dade and Palm Beach counties "could change, or place in doubt the results of the election." Bush lawyer Barry Richard pointed out that there had already been a machine recount of all the ballots, followed by a hand recount that had not included the disputed ballots because they were improperly punched. A third recount,

Here Comes the Judge

As reported by *The New York Times* in November 1998, Judge N. Sanders Sauls, the chief circuit judge in Leon County, "was hauled to the woodshed by the Florida Supreme Court" in what was a "most extraordinary professional humiliation." The justices had received many complaints that he was arrogant and autocratic, ruling over a courthouse bitterly divided by his attitude. Judge Sauls was warned that "things had to change."

The next morning Judge Sauls sent in his letter of resignation. He was promptly removed as chief judge. Two years later, when 59-year-old Judge Sauls was presiding over the recount trial in Tallahassee, five of the seven justices who had chastised him still served on the Florida Supreme Court. No matter how the case in Tallahassee went, both sides had announced that they would appeal if they lost. This meant that Judge Sauls's decision would be reviewed by five of the seven justices who considered him "arbitrary and unfair."

Although a lifelong Democrat, Judge Sauls was appointed to the bench by a Republican governor. Of the 198 cases he has presided over on the Leon County circuit, sixty-one have been reversed on appeal for "taking too narrow an approach with admitting evidence, and for punishing defendants too harshly." He has also received a low rating in local bar association polls.

During the two days of the recount trial, some Democrats felt that Judge Sauls showed prejudice toward Gore's lawyers. With time growing short, he denied their request for a recount of the 14,000 disputed ballots, refusing even to look at them himself to weigh matters involving pregnant and hanging chads. He lost patience with Gore lawyer Stephen Zack while he was interrogating a witness and ordered him to sit down. Sauls was often impatient with Gore's technical witnesses. But Judge Sauls said that a Bush witness, Judge Charles E. Burton, head of the Palm Beach County Canvassing Board, was "a great American."

When the trial ended and Sauls delivered his verdict, a question was immediately raised. Would the Florida Supreme Court affirm Judge Sauls or punish him again? The presidency would hang on the answer.

he said, would be contrary to Florida law. Richard accused the Gore team of demanding "three free shots at the basket" to get the result they wanted.

The arguments narrowed down to whether the condition of the ballots justified their being disallowed or recounted. Expert witnesses for Gore went into great detail about how punch-card balloting could result in hanging chads, which should be counted because they clearly indicated voter intent. This evidence was extremely technical. Many observers, including Judge Sauls, sometimes seemed confused by it.

On the second day of the trial, Bush's lawyers called John Ahmann to the stand as a rebuttal witness. Ahmann had helped develop the Votomatic, the punch-card device used in Miami-Dade and Palm Beach counties. Ahmann

The Votomatic machine

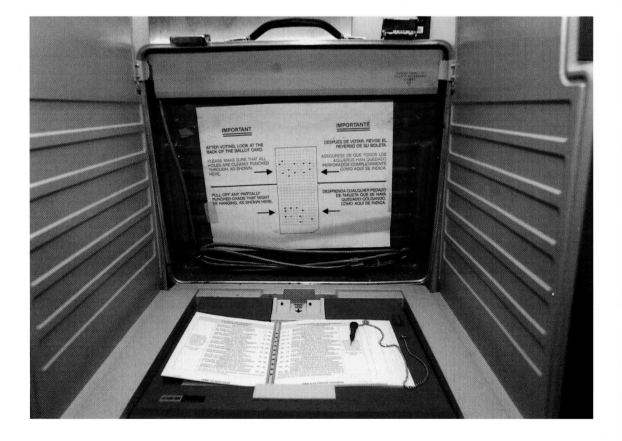

John Ahmann demonstrates the use of his invention in court on December 3.

denied claims by Gore experts that the Votomatic could have produced thousands of paper ballots unreadable by scanners.

There followed a very dramatic moment. Gore lawyer Stephen Zack produced a patent application that Ahmann had submitted twenty years ago for an improved version of the Votomatic. "The surface of the punchboard has become so clogged with chips as to prevent a clean punching operation," Ahmann had stated. "Incompletely punched cards," he had added, "can cause serious errors to occur."

Ahmann also admitted that he had failed to get Miami-Dade to buy a new stylus he had designed to make it less likely for a voter to mispunch a ballot. Ahmann said the one in use was not reliable. Finally, under cross-examination, Ahmann testified that the only sure way to tabulate ballots in "very close elections" was a hand count. This was a key admission. Bush's expert witness had made the central point of Gore's case. Mr. Ahmann was judged by *The New York Times* to be "the Democrats' best witness, even though he was called by the other side."

The Final Decision

On December 4, Judge Sauls ruled that Gore's lawyers had failed to prove "reasonable probability" that the election would turn out differently if the disallowed ballots were recounted. He reasoned that, to be fair, every Florida ballot would have to be recounted by hand—an impractical solution since the Florida legislature had to name the state's Electors by December 12. Gore's lawyers immediately appealed this decision to the Florida Supreme Court.

When, on December 7, the Florida Supreme Court agreed to hear Gore's appeal, the Republican-controlled state legislature called a special session for the next day in order to ratify the Bush Electors certified by Secretary of State Harris. This meant that if the court found for Gore, two Florida slates might be sent to the Electoral College. December 8 loomed as the day of decision.

It began badly for Al Gore. Two verdicts from Seminole and Martin counties concerning altered absentee ballot applications went against him. Seminole County judge Nikki Ann Clark found "no evidence that the request for ballots or the ballots themselves were tainted." Martin County judge Terry Lewis agreed. If the decisions had gone the other way, they would have cost Bush the presidency. When the decisions were read, Bush

Sideshow

The handling of applications for absentee ballots—not the ballots themselves—gave rise to two court cases capable of affecting the results of the election. These applications are mailed out by both parties to registered Republicans and Democrats who vote by mail. Routinely, party officials fill out part of the applications, supplying the ballot identification number required by Florida law. In Seminole and Martin Counties, however, the Republicans neglected to fill in the identification numbers.

When the mistake was realized, Republican Party North Florida Regional Director Michael A. Leach got permission from Seminole County Supervisor of Elections Sandra Gourd, a Republican, to correct the error. Leach used Gourd's office for fifteen days to add identification numbers to Republican ballot applications that had been mailed back. At the same time, incomplete Democratic applications were rejected. A similar scenario played out in Martin County.

Leach altered over 2,000 ballot applications. "I'm a military man; I follow orders," he explained. When his actions were revealed, a local Democrat sued the Seminole County Canvassing Board, demanding that all 15,215 absentee ballots be thrown out. These ballots had gone 2 to 1 for Bush. If they were discarded, he would lose his 4,800-vote lead, and Gore would win the election.

The case was assigned to Leon County Circuit Court Judge Nikki Ann Clark. On November 29, Bush's lawyers asked Judge Clark to disqualify herself because she had once been an aide to the former Democratic governor of Florida, Lawton Chiles, and because Governor Jeb Bush had passed her over for a promotion. She refused. Bush's lawyers appealed her decision, but lost. Meanwhile, on December 1, Democrats also sued the Martin County Canvassing Board for tampering with absentee ballot applications.

On December 6, the same day Judge Clark began hearing the Seminole County case, Al Gore told reporters that altering the applications "doesn't seem fair to me." This was in contrast to his previous insistence that every Florida ballot should be counted. Republicans insisted that correcting the applications was a technicality.

Judge Clark didn't seem to think so. "In a sense," she told Republican lawyers, "what you're telling me is that the Legislature said the person making the request must disclose [the information], but don't worry about it if they don't." Later, when one of the lawyers said "Yes, sir" to her, Judge Clark's tone turned frigid. "I'm not a sir," she informed him.

On December 8, decisions on the Seminole County case and the Martin County case were handed down by Judge Clark and Judge Terry Lewis. The rulings, however, were overwhelmed by the furor raised by a third decision issued the same day. That one triggered the final battle in Election 2000.

supporters chanted "Na, na, na, na, hey, hey, hey goodbye" at Gore supporters.

They were singing another tune later in the day, however, when the Florida Supreme Court handed down its decision overturning Judge Sauls's verdict. In a 4 to 3 vote, the court ordered a recount of disputed ballots. It also ordered "the inclusion of the additional 215 legal votes for Vice President Gore in Palm Beach County and the 168 additional legal votes from Miami-Dade County." These were votes tabulated, but not accepted, before the hand counts stopped.

Florida Supreme Court justice Charles T. Wells, voting with the minority, stated, "I have a deep and abiding concern that the prolonging of the judicial process in the counting contest propels this country and this state into an unprecedented and unnecessary constitutional crisis." Bush lawyers applied for an immediate hearing before the United States Supreme Court. However, because that court had previously seemed reluctant to interfere in a state's electoral process, many observers felt that the Florida decision had made Al Gore the next president of the United States.

On December 9, by a 5 to 4 vote, the United States Supreme Court agreed to hear Bush's appeal. Two days later, the court heard arguments from, and put questions to, lawyers from both sides. The justices' questions spotlighted the issues on which they would base their decision. Justice Anthony Kennedy was concerned about justifying "our federal jurisdiction." Justice Stephen G. Breyer raised the question of what "would be a fair standard" for hand counting disputed ballots. Justice David Souter was disturbed that there was not "one objective rule for all counties" in counting ballots. Justice Sandra Day O'Connor wondered if the court did not have to "give special deference to the [state] legislature's choices insofar as a presidential election is concerned." The questioning and oral arguments lasted ninety minutes.

On December 19, George W. Bush and Al Gore met at the vice presidential residence in Washington. The meeting between the fierce competitors lasted only fifteen minutes.

At 10 P.M. on December 12, the United States Supreme Court ruled on the case. By a margin of 5 to 4, it overturned the Florida Supreme Court's decision to hand count the disputed ballots. The majority ruled that it would be impossible to recount the votes in a way that could both meet "minimal constitutional standards" and be accomplished within the deadline.

The next day, Al Gore conceded the election. George W. Bush was now the next president of the United States. So ended the most extraordinary United States presidential election in over one hundred years.

Afterword . . .

Many questions were raised by the 2000 presidential election. Did the system fail? Should the Electoral College be scrapped? Should it be retained, but reformed? Should it be kept as is? Was the election stolen? Is a certain amount of vote stealing inevitable in every election? Should election procedures and voting machines be standardized throughout the country regardless of the huge expense involved? Should restrictions on hand recounts be relaxed? Should the judiciary have a lesser or greater role in deciding election conflicts?

All of these questions and more were raised, and often raised loudly, during the thirty-six days between Election Day and the decision by the United States Supreme Court confirming George W. Bush as the president-elect. Loud demands for changes and reforms were made by politicians, the media, and a frustrated public. As the months went by, however, the clamor to act subsided. Congress was occupied with campaign finance reform, the national budget, and tax reduction. The media was focused on other, more immediate stories. The public was concerned with the down-spiraling stock market. The hubbub over the electoral process died down to barely a murmur.

Some changes may be made—or not. It's doubtful that there will be any kind of major overhaul of the voting process in the foreseeable future. We will probably go on electing presidents pretty much as we always have. It's an imperfect method, but it is democratic. After all, as a wise man once observed, democracy is the worst of systems—except for all the others.

Chronology

Nov. 7, 2000	7:47 P.M. Media declares that presidential candidate Al Gore has won Florida.
	9:54 P.M. Networks acknowledge mistake; Florida is still undecided.
Nov. 8	2:18 A.M. Media announces that George W. Bush has won Florida and the presidency.
	4:00 A.M. Networks announce that Florida vote and presidency are still undecided.
	Suit filed to throw out Palm Beach County results because of butterfly ballot.
Nov. 12	Palm Beach electoral officials agree to hand recount 462,657 ballots.
Nov. 13	Florida Secretary of State Katherine Harris rules counting must stop by 5 P.M. next day.
Nov. 15	Broward, Dade, and Palm Beach counties submit reasons hand count should resume. Harris rejects their arguments. Broward resumes hand count anyway.
Nov. 16	Florida Supreme Court rules hand counts can go forward.
Nov. 22	Florida Supreme Court extends deadline for Secretary Harris to accept hand recount totals.
Nov. 26	Harris declares Bush the winner in Florida by 537 votes.
Dec. 1	U.S. Supreme Court hears arguments over allowing hand counts to proceed.

Dec. 2	Trial over counting chads opens in Tallahassee.
Dec. 4	Judge rules in favor of Bush in Tallahassee chad trial.
	U.S. Supreme Court avoids ruling on hand counts and sends case back to Florida Supreme Court for clarification.
Dec. 8	Gore loses appeals to have Republican absentee ballots thrown out in Seminole and Martin counties.
	Gore scores huge victory when Florida Supreme Court reverses Tallahassee verdict and orders recount of disputed ballots.
Dec. 12	U.S. Supreme Court overturns Florida Supreme Court decision, effectively sealing the election for Bush.
Dec. 13	Gore concedes the election to Bush.

For Further Reading

Andryszewski, Tricia. *The Reform Party: Ross Perot and Pat Buchanan.* Brookfield, CT: The Millbrook Press, 2000.

Bowen, Nancy. *Ralph Nader: A Man with a Mission.* Brookfield, CT: The Millbrook Press, 2002.

Feinberg, Barbara Silberdick. *Electing the President.* Brookfield, CT: The Millbrook Press, 1995.

Greenfield, Jeff. *Oh, Waiter! One Order of Crow: Inside the Strangest Presidential Election Finish in American History.* New York: Putnam Publishing Group, 2001.

Morin, Isobel V. *Politics, American Style: Political Parties in American History.* Brookfield, CT: The Millbrook Press, 1999.

Simon, Roger. *Divided We Stand: How Al Gore Beat George Bush and Lost the Presidency.* New York: Times Books, 2001.

Toobin, Jeffrey. *Too Close to Call.* New York: Random House, 2001.

Index